★ THE ★
UNITED STATES
PRESIDENTS

WILLIAM
TAFT

BreAnn Rumsch

**Checkerboard
Library**

An Imprint of Abdo Publishing
abdobooks.com

ABDOBOOKS.COM

Published by Abdo Publishing, a division of ABDO, PO Box 398166, Minneapolis, Minnesota 55439. Copyright © 2021 by Abdo Consulting Group, Inc. International copyrights reserved in all countries. No part of this book may be reproduced in any form without written permission from the publisher. Checkerboard Library™ is a trademark and logo of Abdo Publishing.

Printed in the United States of America, North Mankato, Minnesota
052020
092020

THIS BOOK CONTAINS
RECYCLED MATERIALS

Design: Emily O'Malley, Kelly Doudna, Mighty Media, Inc.
Production: Mighty Media, Inc.
Editor: Jessica Rusick

Cover Photograph: Stock Montage/Getty Images
Interior Photographs: Albert de Bruijn/iStockphoto, p. 37; AP Images, pp. 7 (Chief Justice Taft), 33, 36; Getty Images, pp. 11, 14, 17, 21, 22, 23, 32; Hulton Archive/Getty Images, p. 29; Library of Congress, pp. 6, 7, 10, 13, 15, 19, 24, 27, 28, 40; MPI/Getty Images, p. 12; North Wind Picture Archives, p. 25; Pete Souza/Flickr, p. 44; Shutterstock Images, pp. 38, 39; Topical Press Agency/Getty Images, pp. 5, 18; Underwood and Underwood/Getty Images, p. 31; Wikimedia Commons, pp. 40 (Washington), 42

Library of Congress Control Number: 2019956553

Publisher's Cataloging-in-Publication Data
Names: Rumsch, BreAnn, author.
Title: William Taft / by BreAnn Rumsch
Description: Minneapolis, Minnesota : Abdo Publishing, 2021 | Series: The United States presidents | Includes online resources and index.
Identifiers: ISBN 9781532193736 (lib. bdg.) | ISBN 9781098212377 (ebook)
Subjects: LCSH: Taft, William H. (William Howard), 1857-1930--Juvenile literature. | Presidents--Biography--Juvenile literature. | Presidents--United States--History--Juvenile literature. | Legislators--United States--Biography--Juvenile literature. | Politics and government--Biography--Juvenile literature.
Classification: DDC 973.912092--dc23

★ CONTENTS ★

William Taft

William Taft was the twenty-seventh president of the United States. He also served as **chief justice** of the US **Supreme Court**. Taft is the only person in US history to have held both offices.

Taft came from a wealthy family. They helped him get a good education. Taft attended Yale University and the Cincinnati Law School.

For most of his life, Taft worked as a lawyer and a judge. He also served as governor of the Philippines. Under President Theodore Roosevelt, Taft also worked as **secretary of war**.

In 1908, Americans elected Taft president. While in office, he broke up **trusts** and worked to lower **tariffs**. During this time, the **Republican** Party was divided. Taft tried to work with both sides of the party. But they could not get along.

Taft lost the next presidential election to Woodrow Wilson. After leaving the White House, Taft became a professor at Yale. Then, he was appointed chief justice of the Supreme Court. Taft was honored to take the position, and he served his country well.

★ TIMELINE ★

1886

On June 19, Taft married Helen "Nellie" Herron.

1878

Taft graduated second in his class from Yale University in Connecticut.

1892

Taft became a judge on the US Circuit Court of Appeals for the Sixth Circuit.

1857

William Howard Taft was born on September 15 in Cincinnati, Ohio.

1880

Taft graduated from Cincinnati Law School in Ohio.

1874

Taft graduated from high school.

1881

Taft became an assistant prosecuting attorney in Hamilton County, Ohio.

1890

President Benjamin Harrison appointed Taft US solicitor general.

1887

Taft became a judge on the Ohio Superior Court.

Will's birthplace in Cincinnati, Ohio

Will attended local schools. Schoolwork was not easy for him, so he had to study hard. And, Will's classmates made fun of him because he was large. They even called him "Lubber." Despite the teasing, Will had many friends.

In 1874, Will graduated from high school. Then he attended Yale University in Connecticut. In 1878, Will graduated second in his class. All his hard studying had paid off.

Work and Family

After graduating from Yale, Taft decided to become a lawyer. He attended the Cincinnati Law School in Ohio and graduated in 1880.

In 1881, Taft became an assistant **prosecuting attorney** in Hamilton County, Ohio. He also worked for a short time as a collector of **internal revenue**.

Several years before, Taft had met Helen "Nellie" Herron. She was the daughter of a well-known lawyer. The couple married on June 19, 1886.

In 1887, Taft became a judge on the Cincinnati **Superior Court**. He

Helen Herron Taft

greatly enjoyed his work. Taft dreamed of one day becoming a US **Supreme Court** justice.

The Tafts soon decided to start a family. They welcomed their first child, Robert, in 1889. Later, the Tafts had two more children. Helen was born in 1891, and Charles followed in 1897.

In 1890, President Benjamin Harrison asked Taft to be the new US **solicitor general**. Taft accepted the job. As solicitor general, Taft was able to argue cases before the Supreme Court.

President Benjamin Harrison

Two years later, President Harrison gave Taft a new job. Taft served as a judge on the US **Circuit Court** of Appeals for the Sixth Circuit. He kept this job for eight years. During this time, Taft was also **dean** of the Cincinnati Law School.

Governor Taft

In 1898, the Philippine Islands became a US territory. In 1900, President William McKinley sent Taft there to establish order and form a government. The next year, Taft became the first **civil** governor of the Philippines.

Governor Taft (*center*) worked with a commission to establish a new government and laws in the Philippines.

Governor Taft did much for the Filipino people. He built roads, harbors, and schools. And he developed a court system. He also worked for land reforms and an improved **economy**. Taft hoped that one day the Filipinos would run their own government. Independence eventually came to them in 1946.

Mr. and Mrs. Taft (*center*) traveled to the Philippines by boat.

The Tafts enjoyed the Philippines. They lived on a large estate with many servants. There, they held numerous dinners, parties, and balls.

In 1902, President Theodore Roosevelt asked Taft to be a US **Supreme Court** judge. Taft had always wanted this job, but he did not take it. He felt his work in the Philippines was unfinished.

The Filipinos did not want Taft to leave, either. They approved of his gentle leadership. And Mrs. Taft loved her grand life on the islands.

15

Secretary Taft

In 1903, President Roosevelt asked Taft to be his **secretary of war.** This time, Mrs. Taft encouraged her husband to take the job. But Taft said he had "no love for American politics." He was also unsure if he was right for the position. Yet, Roosevelt eventually convinced Taft to join his **cabinet**.

That year, the United States and Panama made a treaty. It said the United States could construct the **Panama Canal**. The United States would also control an area of land around the construction site. This was called the Canal Zone.

In 1904, Taft returned to Washington, DC, to begin work as secretary of war. During this time, he oversaw the construction of the Panama Canal. Taft also worked to establish a government in the Canal Zone.

Roosevelt and Taft worked well together. The president often assigned Taft to special tasks. President Roosevelt felt that everything was running well in Washington. He said that was because Taft was "sitting on the lid."

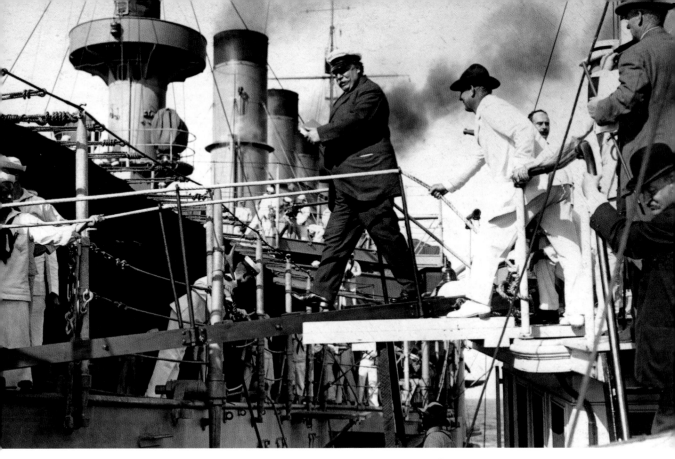

Taft (*center*) often traveled to Panama to inspect the construction of the Panama Canal.

As **secretary of war**, Taft traveled often. He visited Japan to help Roosevelt work on the Treaty of Portsmouth. This treaty ended the **Russo-Japanese War** in 1905. He also traveled to Cuba in 1906. There, he helped stop a revolution from breaking out.

Roosevelt and Taft

In 1908, Roosevelt announced that he would not seek reelection. He recommended Taft as the **Republican** candidate. At first, Taft objected. He hoped to join the **Supreme Court** instead. But Taft's wife and brothers convinced him to run for president.

Taft easily won the Republican nomination. New York representative James S. Sherman was chosen as his **running mate**. Their opponents were **Democrat** William Jennings Bryan and his running mate, John W. Kern. Taft easily won the election.

A campaign poster for Taft
promised voters "Good Times."

President Taft

Taft took office on March 4, 1909. He still had doubts about being president. Taft knew he could not be another Roosevelt. "Our ways are different," he said. Taft decided to take Roosevelt's ideas and try to make them better.

However, Taft had trouble from the start. The **Republican** Party was divided when Taft took office. This made it difficult to pass laws.

Taft wanted Congress to lower **tariffs**. The House of Representatives had many **liberal** Republicans. They quickly passed a bill that lowered numerous tariffs. Then, the bill went to the Senate. There, **conservative** Republicans made many changes to the bill. Their changes kept tariffs high on most items.

Despite these changes, President Taft signed the Payne-Aldrich Tariff Act into law in 1909. The law did not lower as many tariffs as Taft

SUPREME COURT APPOINTMENTS

HORACE H. LURTON: 1910

CHARLES EVANS HUGHES: 1910

WILLIS VAN DEVANTER: 1911

JOSEPH R. LAMAR: 1911

EDWARD DOUGLASS WHITE: 1910
(promoted to Chief Justice)

MAHLON PITNEY: 1912

Taft was the first president to own a car. However, he and his wife rode to the inauguration ceremony in a horse-drawn carriage.

had promised. Still, Taft justified the law in public. This angered **liberal Republicans**. They felt President Taft had gone back on his word.

In May, President Taft's wife had a **stroke**. She was too sick to be a hostess at the White House. So, their daughter Helen often did this job. Taft missed his wife's help after she became ill. He had relied on her keen political advice.

Soon, more trouble followed. Gifford Pinchot was chief

of the US Forest Service. In late 1909, he accused **Secretary of the Interior** Richard A. Ballinger and Taft of making dishonest land deals. A special group of congressmen cleared Ballinger and Taft. The following year, Taft fired Pinchot.

However, liberal Republicans believed Pinchot's claims. They grew unhappy with Taft. They began to turn to former president Roosevelt as their true leader.

In 1910, Roosevelt began making many liberal speeches.

—— **Gifford Pinchot** ——

Taft and his daughter, Helen

He talked about a "New Nationalism." He stood for honest government, social justice, and increased welfare.

Roosevelt's speeches upset many **conservative Republicans**. They sided with President Taft against Roosevelt. The Republican Party split in two. Conservative Republicans supported Taft. **Liberal** Republicans supported Roosevelt.

Despite his troubles with the Republican Party, Taft had some success with Congress. He helped form the **Tariff** Board and broke up many **trusts**. Taft also took the first steps toward establishing a federal budget.

In 1912, Taft established the US Children's Bureau. This agency oversaw child welfare. That same year, Taft made Arizona and New Mexico US states. And, Alaska became a US territory.

The US Children's Bureau was the first federal agency in the world to focus on helping children and families.

President Taft signed an act to approve Arizona's statehood.

PRESIDENT TAFT'S CABINET

ONE TERM
March 4, 1909–March 4, 1913

- ★ **STATE:** Philander C. Knox
- ★ **TREASURY:** Franklin MacVeagh
- ★ **WAR:** Jacob M. Dickinson
  Henry L. Stimson (from May 22, 1911)
- ★ **NAVY:** George von Lengerke Meyer
- ★ **ATTORNEY GENERAL:** George W. Wickersham
- ★ **INTERIOR:** Richard A. Ballinger
  Walter L. Fisher (from March 7, 1911)
- ★ **AGRICULTURE:** James Wilson
- ★ **COMMERCE AND LABOR:** Charles Nagel

President William Taft

A Tough Campaign

In 1912, **conservative Republicans** nominated President Taft to run for a second term. Sherman was renominated for vice president. Roosevelt and the **liberal** Republicans organized the **Progressive** Party. The party nominated Roosevelt for president. His **running mate** was California governor Hiram W. Johnson.

A newspaper reporter asked Roosevelt how he felt about his election chances. Roosevelt replied that he felt "as strong as a bull moose." The new Progressive Party was soon nicknamed the Bull Moose Party.

The **Democratic** Party nominated Governor Woodrow Wilson of New Jersey. Indiana governor Thomas R. Marshall became his running mate. With the Republican Party split in two, it had little power. So, Wilson easily won the election.

Woodrow Wilson

Taft made many speeches while campaigning against Roosevelt and Wilson.

Chief Justice

Taft left the White House in 1913. He then became a law professor at Yale. During these years, he continued to follow politics in Washington, DC. And he often gave speeches.

America entered **World War I** in 1917. The next year, Taft helped lead the National War Labor Board. It improved relations between American businesses and their workers. This helped produce more goods for the war.

In 1921, President Warren G. Harding asked Taft to be **chief justice** of the US **Supreme Court**. Taft was honored to accept. He is the only president to have held this position.

When Taft joined the Supreme Court, it was overloaded with cases. So, he asked Congress to pass the Judges Act. It would give the Supreme Court more freedom in choosing its cases. This would rid the court of backed-up cases and let it run smoothly. Congress passed the Judges Act in 1925.

Chief Justice Taft did other important work too. He helped win approval for a new Supreme Court building.

Chief Justice Taft (*seated, center*) with his
associate justices. The US Supreme Court has
one chief justice and eight associate justices.

The building is still used today. Taft also wrote **opinions** on
253 court cases.

In February 1930, Taft retired from the **Supreme Court**.
On March 8, William Taft died from heart problems. He
was buried in Arlington National Cemetery in Virginia.

As president, Taft wanted to lower **tariffs**, end **trusts**, and establish a federal budget. He was successful with many of these projects. But Taft's term was marked by fighting within the **Republican** Party. This weakened Taft's power as president. Yet as **chief justice**, William Taft made many important contributions to his country.

Taft oversaw the planning and initial construction of the US Supreme Court building in Washington, DC.

Chief Justice Taft served on the Supreme Court from 1921 to 1930.

BRANCHES OF GOVERNMENT

The US government is divided into three branches. They are the executive, legislative, and judicial branches. This division is called a separation of powers. Each branch has some power over the others. This is called a system of checks and balances.

★ EXECUTIVE BRANCH

The executive branch enforces laws. It is made up of the president, the vice president, and the president's cabinet. The president represents the United States around the world. He or she oversees relations with other countries and signs treaties. The president signs bills into law and appoints officials and federal judges. He or she also leads the military and manages government workers.

★ LEGISLATIVE BRANCH

The legislative branch makes laws, maintains the military, and regulates trade. It also has the power to declare war. This branch consists of the Senate and the House of Representatives. Together, these two houses make up Congress. Each state has two senators. A state's population determines the number of representatives it has.

★ JUDICIAL BRANCH

The judicial branch interprets laws. It consists of district courts, courts of appeals, and the Supreme Court. District courts try cases. If a person disagrees with a trial's outcome, he or she may appeal. If a court of appeals supports the ruling, a person may appeal to the Supreme Court. The Supreme Court also makes sure that laws follow the US Constitution.

THE PRESIDENT ★

★ QUALIFICATIONS FOR OFFICE

To be president, a person must meet three requirements. A candidate must be at least 35 years old and a natural-born US citizen. He or she must also have lived in the United States for at least 14 years.

★ ELECTORAL COLLEGE

The US presidential election is an indirect election. Voters from each state choose electors to represent them in the Electoral College. The number of electors from each state is based on the state's population. Each elector has one electoral vote. Electors are pledged to cast their vote for the candidate who receives the highest number of popular votes in their state. A candidate must receive the majority of Electoral College votes to win.

★ TERM OF OFFICE

Each president may be elected to two four-year terms. Sometimes, a president may only be elected once. This happens if he or she served more than two years of the previous president's term.

The presidential election is held on the Tuesday after the first Monday in November. The president is sworn in on January 20 of the following year. At that time, he or she takes the oath of office:

> *I do solemnly swear (or affirm) that I will faithfully execute the office of President of the United States, and will to the best of my ability, preserve, protect and defend the Constitution of the United States.*

LINE OF SUCCESSION

The Presidential Succession Act of 1947 defines who becomes president if the president cannot serve. The vice president is first in the line of succession. Next are the Speaker of the House and the President Pro Tempore of the Senate. If none of these individuals is able to serve, the office falls to the president's cabinet members. They would take office in the order in which each department was created:

Secretary of State

Secretary of the Treasury

Secretary of Defense

Attorney General

Secretary of the Interior

Secretary of Agriculture

Secretary of Commerce

Secretary of Labor

Secretary of Health and Human Services

Secretary of Housing and Urban Development

Secretary of Transportation

Secretary of Energy

Secretary of Education

Secretary of Veterans Affairs

Secretary of Homeland Security

While in office, the president receives a salary of $400,000 each year. He or she lives in the White House and has 24-hour Secret Service protection.

The president may travel on a Boeing 747 jet called Air Force One. The airplane can accommodate 76 passengers. It has kitchens, a dining room, sleeping areas, and a conference room. It also has fully equipped offices with the latest communications systems. Air Force One can fly halfway around the world before needing to refuel. It can even refuel in flight!

Air Force One

If the president wishes to travel by car, he or she uses Cadillac One. It has been modified with heavy armor and communications systems. The president takes

Cadillac One

Cadillac One along when visiting other countries if secure transportation will be needed.

The president also travels on a helicopter called Marine One. Like the presidential car, Marine One accompanies the president when traveling abroad if necessary.

Sometimes, the president needs to get away and relax with family and friends. Camp David is the official presidential retreat. It is located in the cool, wooded mountains of Maryland. The US Navy maintains the retreat, and the US Marine Corps keeps it secure. The camp offers swimming, tennis, golf, and hiking.

When the president leaves office, he or she receives lifetime Secret Service protection. He or she also receives a yearly pension of $207,800 and funding for office space, supplies, and staff.

Marine One

George Washington

Abraham Lincoln

Theodore Roosevelt

	PRESIDENT	PARTY	TOOK OFFICE
1	George Washington	None	April 30, 1789
2	John Adams	Federalist	March 4, 1797
3	Thomas Jefferson	Democratic-Republican	March 4, 1801
4	James Madison	Democratic-Republican	March 4, 1809
5	James Monroe	Democratic-Republican	March 4, 1817
6	John Quincy Adams	Democratic-Republican	March 4, 1825
7	Andrew Jackson	Democrat	March 4, 1829
8	Martin Van Buren	Democrat	March 4, 1837
9	William H. Harrison	Whig	March 4, 1841
10	John Tyler	Whig	April 6, 1841
11	James K. Polk	Democrat	March 4, 1845
12	Zachary Taylor	Whig	March 5, 1849
13	Millard Fillmore	Whig	July 10, 1850
14	Franklin Pierce	Democrat	March 4, 1853
15	James Buchanan	Democrat	March 4, 1857
16	Abraham Lincoln	Republican	March 4, 1861
17	Andrew Johnson	Democrat	April 15, 1865
18	Ulysses S. Grant	Republican	March 4, 1869
19	Rutherford B. Hayes	Republican	March 3, 1877

LEFT OFFICE	TERMS SERVED	VICE PRESIDENT
March 4, 1797	Two	John Adams
March 4, 1801	One	Thomas Jefferson
March 4, 1809	Two	Aaron Burr, George Clinton
March 4, 1817	Two	George Clinton, Elbridge Gerry
March 4, 1825	Two	Daniel D. Tompkins
March 4, 1829	One	John C. Calhoun
March 4, 1837	Two	John C. Calhoun, Martin Van Buren
March 4, 1841	One	Richard M. Johnson
April 4, 1841	Died During First Term	John Tyler
March 4, 1845	Completed Harrison's Term	Office Vacant
March 4, 1849	One	George M. Dallas
July 9, 1850	Died During First Term	Millard Fillmore
March 4, 1853	Completed Taylor's Term	Office Vacant
March 4, 1857	One	William R.D. King
March 4, 1861	One	John C. Breckinridge
April 15, 1865	Served One Term, Died During Second Term	Hannibal Hamlin, Andrew Johnson
March 4, 1869	Completed Lincoln's Second Term	Office Vacant
March 4, 1877	Two	Schuyler Colfax, Henry Wilson
March 4, 1881	One	William A. Wheeler

PRESIDENT		PARTY	TOOK OFFICE
20	James A. Garfield	Republican	March 4, 1881
21	Chester Arthur	Republican	September 20, 1881
22	Grover Cleveland	Democrat	March 4, 1885
23	Benjamin Harrison	Republican	March 4, 1889
24	Grover Cleveland	Democrat	March 4, 1893
25	William McKinley	Republican	March 4, 1897
26	Theodore Roosevelt	Republican	September 14, 1901
27	William Taft	Republican	March 4, 1909
28	Woodrow Wilson	Democrat	March 4, 1913
29	Warren G. Harding	Republican	March 4, 1921
30	Calvin Coolidge	Republican	August 3, 1923
31	Herbert Hoover	Republican	March 4, 1929
32	Franklin D. Roosevelt	Democrat	March 4, 1933
33	Harry S. Truman	Democrat	April 12, 1945
34	Dwight D. Eisenhower	Republican	January 20, 1953
35	John F. Kennedy	Democrat	January 20, 1961

Franklin D. Roosevelt

John F. Kennedy

Ronald Reagan

LEFT OFFICE	TERMS SERVED	VICE PRESIDENT
September 19, 1881	Died During First Term	Chester Arthur
March 4, 1885	Completed Garfield's Term	Office Vacant
March 4, 1889	One	Thomas A. Hendricks
March 4, 1893	One	Levi P. Morton
March 4, 1897	One	Adlai E. Stevenson
September 14, 1901	Served One Term, Died During Second Term	Garret A. Hobart, Theodore Roosevelt
March 4, 1909	Completed McKinley's Second Term, Served One Term	Office Vacant, Charles Fairbanks
March 4, 1913	One	James S. Sherman
March 4, 1921	Two	Thomas R. Marshall
August 2, 1923	Died During First Term	Calvin Coolidge
March 4, 1929	Completed Harding's Term, Served One Term	Office Vacant, Charles Dawes
March 4, 1933	One	Charles Curtis
April 12, 1945	Served Three Terms, Died During Fourth Term	John Nance Garner, Henry A. Wallace, Harry S. Truman
January 20, 1953	Completed Roosevelt's Fourth Term, Served One Term	Office Vacant, Alben Barkley
January 20, 1961	Two	Richard Nixon
November 22, 1963	Died During First Term	Lyndon B. Johnson

	PRESIDENT	PARTY	TOOK OFFICE
36	Lyndon B. Johnson	Democrat	November 22, 1963
37	Richard Nixon	Republican	January 20, 1969
38	Gerald Ford	Republican	August 9, 1974
39	Jimmy Carter	Democrat	January 20, 1977
40	Ronald Reagan	Republican	January 20, 1981
41	George H.W. Bush	Republican	January 20, 1989
42	Bill Clinton	Democrat	January 20, 1993
43	George W. Bush	Republican	January 20, 2001
44	Barack Obama	Democrat	January 20, 2009
45	Donald Trump	Republican	January 20, 2017

Barack Obama

★ PRESIDENTS MATH GAME ★

Have fun with this presidents math game! First, study the list above and memorize each president's name and number. Then, use math to figure out which president completes each equation below.

1. William Taft − James Monroe = ?

2. Thomas Jefferson + William Taft = ?

3. William Taft − George Washington = ?

Answers: 1. Grover Cleveland (27 − 5 = 22)
2. Calvin Coolidge (3 + 27 = 30)
3. Theodore Roosevelt (27 − 1 = 26)

LEFT OFFICE	TERMS SERVED	VICE PRESIDENT
January 20, 1969	Completed Kennedy's Term, Served One Term	Office Vacant, Hubert H. Humphrey
August 9, 1974	Completed First Term, Resigned During Second Term	Spiro T. Agnew, Gerald Ford
January 20, 1977	Completed Nixon's Second Term	Nelson A. Rockefeller
January 20, 1981	One	Walter Mondale
January 20, 1989	Two	George H.W. Bush
January 20, 1993	One	Dan Quayle
January 20, 2001	Two	Al Gore
January 20, 2009	Two	Dick Cheney
January 20, 2017	Two	Joe Biden
		Mike Pence

★ WRITE TO THE PRESIDENT ★

You may write to the president at:

The White House
1600 Pennsylvania Avenue NW
Washington, DC 20500

You may email the president at:

www.whitehouse.gov/contact

★ GLOSSARY ★

cabinet—a group of advisers chosen by the president to lead government departments.

chief justice—the head judge of the US Supreme Court. A justice is a judge on the US Supreme Court.

circuit court—a court whose judges hold, or used to hold, court first at one place, then at another, in regular sequence through a district.

civil—of or relating to the state or its citizens.

conservative—a person who has traditional beliefs and often dislikes change.

dean—a person at a university who is in charge of guiding students.

Democrat—a member of the Democratic political party. When William Taft was president, Democrats supported farmers and landowners.

economy—the way a nation uses its money, goods, and natural resources.

internal revenue—the income, such as taxes, that a government collects from its citizens.

liberal—a person who favors change and progress.

opinion—a legal explanation of a judge's decision on a particular case.

Panama Canal—a human-made, narrow canal across Panama that connects the Atlantic and Pacific oceans.

Progressive—a member of one of several Progressive political parties organized in the United States. Progressives believed in liberal social, political, and economic reform.

prosecuting attorney—a lawyer who represents the government in criminal cases.

Republican—a member of the Republican political party. Republicans are conservative and believe in small government.

running mate—a candidate running for a lower-rank position on an election ticket, especially the candidate for vice president.

Russo-Japanese War—from 1904 to 1905. A war between Russia and Japan. They fought for control of Korea and Manchuria.

secretary of the interior—a member of the president's cabinet who manages public lands and protects wildlife.

secretary of war—a member of the president's cabinet who handles the nation's defense. This position was replaced by the secretary of the army in 1947.

solicitor general—a law officer, whose main job is to assist an attorney general. In the United States, the solicitor general represents the government in Supreme Court cases.

stroke—a sudden loss of consciousness, sensation, and voluntary motion. This attack of paralysis is caused by a rupture to a blood vessel of the brain, often caused by a blood clot.

superior court—a court in some states that sits above the courts of limited or special authority, and below the court or courts of appeal.

Supreme Court—the highest, most powerful court in the United States.

tariff—the taxes a government puts on imported or exported goods.

trust—a group of companies joined by a legal agreement, which stops competition over a good or a service.

World War I—from 1914 to 1918, fought in Europe. Great Britain, France, Russia, the United States, and their allies were on one side. Germany, Austria-Hungary, and their allies were on the other side.

ONLINE RESOURCES

To learn more about William Taft, please visit **abdobooklinks.com** or scan this QR code. These links are routinely monitored and updated to provide the most current information available.

★ INDEX ★